On Crumbled Pieces of Paper

Ebony Holmes

BookLeaf Publishing

India | USA | UK

Presentation by *BookLeaf Publishing*

Web: www.bookleafpub.com

E-mail: info@bookleafpub.com

ISBN: 9789363303171

First edition 2024

To my Mom, you always knew I could.

Thanks for always having faith in me and

*celebrating me as a writer long before
publication.*

ACKNOWLEDGMENT

Thank you to Bookleaf Publishing for giving me the opportunity to write this book and for publishing it. It's been a long-time dream of mine. I look forward to working with you in the future.

Thank you to my husband, Aj, who supports me in everything I do.

Thank you to my parents Jessie and Odetta for always pushing me.

To my siblings Ivory, Meladie, Jessie Jr., and Christine. Thanks for proofreading, editing, and giving feedback on all my writings.

To my grandma, who is my greatest example of living a balanced life. To My Godmom, who has always helped me in every way possible. To everyone who has supported me, loved me, or encouraged me to go after what I desire.

I couldn't do it without any of you.

Lastly, to my two heartbeats, Tony and Calvin. I love you to the moon and back.

Watching the two of you grow is my greatest joy.

On Crumbled Pieces of Paper

On crumbled pieces of paper where I jot down
my thoughts
Some words that I wouldn't want you to seek
My most inner, deepest thoughts
Thoughts so deep that they choke me when I
speak
From my brain to this paper through closed lips
and sometimes watered eyes
From the heaviest of hearts, from the jungle of
my mind
I jot down these words to drop the heaviest of
weights
Weights that block me from what I want to say
Block me from the peace of mind I do seek
Speak girl, speak, but my voice is silent
Think girl, think, but I can't so I write
I write to get it out
I write so you may know
I write so I can laugh
I write to keep from crying
I write to remember how I feel
I write to feel free
I write and I write—on crumbled pieces of paper

The Ocean

The ocean whispered clearly to me.
Oh, I listened but was unable to speak.
She spoke to me calmly and in peace.
She called my name for perpetuity.

The ocean outstretched wide for me.
Her wave rose up but reached me not.
Though on the shore I saw her arms.
Yet I dare not avail myself to thee.

The ocean provided nourishment for me.
She fed my body, mind, and soul.
Her sustenance was fuel for my ambition,
As I indulged in her succulent delight.

The ocean's wind saluted me.
It caressed my sun-kissed cheeks.
The gentle peck of the salt-foamed blue,
Destined to lead me through to paradise.

In My Dreams

I see it in my dreams
Just as plain as day,
But it doesn't occur to me
That it won't turn out that way.

I see it in my dreams
Where I want to go,
But exactly how to get there
I really don't know.

I see it in my dreams
What road I need to take,
But not knowingly
I make a mistake.

I see what I want to do
And where I want to go,
But it's never as it seems
The way I see it in my dreams.

Stormy Weather

It's just like the rain
On my window pane
No matter what I try to do.
I can't escape what I'm going through.

It's like stepping out into a storm,
Hoping you come back with no harm.
Seeing the lightning sharp,
Praying it doesn't break your heart.

Just remember, stand tall and don't bend,
Cause there's always a point,
When the storm must end.

Life's Hard

I was born by the river in a little tent.
        Tent?
Naw, I really wasn't. I'm just here to vent.
Yeah, at times life is too hard.
No, I'm not afraid to die.
I'm just not ready to leave.
I've been hoping and praying.
Waiting for my change to come.
Crying and wondering,
Lord, when the pain gonna stop?
No, this pain ain't so much physical.
Sometimes it's more of a mental
breakdown in the communication
between the natural and the spiritual.
Lord your will is where I want to be,
but you know my flesh is weak.
Getting up early to pray and read your word,
but fell right back to sleep.
So, I don't even know if you heard,
the words of my requests,
the calls of my distress.
Living this life seems to cause so much stress.
But I'm not stressing it,
I'm searching for the blessing in it.
Every storm that I face,

I pray the Lord gives me grace.
To pass all these tests.
So, I can continue to run this race.
With my feet planted firmly in place.
No, I won't get weary.
Best believe I won't faint.
Because the joy of the Lord is my strength.
I'm naming it and claiming it until the end
of my race when I can clearly say.
It's finished. I'm finished.
I've won!

I Pray, Dear Lord, Today

In a day and time like this.
I can only ask for one thing.
Dear lord, I pray today that you
will keep me close to you?
I don't want to be one of the lost.
It is my desire to be pure and true.

My life forever I want to spend with you.
You and me from now to eternity.
I'm taking the steps to walk like you.
Learning the language to talk like you.

I love you more than life itself.
Cause when I found you, I've found myself,
and now I'm blessed.

So, grant, dear lord, this prayer I pray today,
Allow me to be like you in every way.
To walk and talk and look like you.
To pray, to live, to act just like you.

Happy And You Know It

If you're happy and you know it
Raise your hands in the air.
Shout out loud, tell the whole world
That you're glad to be here.

There's no better place you could be.
Show the whole world there's more to see.
A life full of love with family and friends.
You can ask someone else if you don't believe
me.

If you're happy and you know it
Don't be ashamed to show it.
Let the people know exactly how you feel.
So don't blow your chance to be real.

Show the world that you love it here.
Let them know that you're not afraid to show it.
Tell them that you're happy and you know it

For Gram

Yesterday started without you.
Tomorrow will do the same.
God saw that you were tired,
Therefore, He called your name.

We're left with just our memories,
and some pictures in their frames.
Times of joy, smiles, and laughter
sorrow, heartache, and pain.

You taught me how to love
You showed me that you cared.
I could always count on you to be real,
Never hiding how you feel.

Gram, as time goes on without you.
How empty our world seems.
But, knowing you're in a better place,
Puts our hearts and minds at ease.

It's time now for you to rest
So go in peace; you've earned your sleep.

And when tomorrow starts without you,
We won't think you're far apart
For every time we think of you,
You're right here in our hearts.

Not Today

The alarm sounded as it does every day
but I turned it off and rolled right back over
cause I am not getting up today.

My phone ranged and though I answered it
I just laid there, not saying a word; I just listened
to what they had to say cause I am not with it
today.

I hear the kids, they are awake now. They
peeped their heads in to say good morning.
I tell them to brush their teeth and get breakfast.
Yes you can play your electronics
Cause I am not getting up today.

The laundry will wait for another day.
The cleaning won't get done today.
The kids will have to pick up after themselves.
Cause I am just not with it today.

I turned on the T.V., no show in particular. I
snuggled into my pillow, I cover my head
with my blanket and close my eyes
Cause I am not getting up today.

O me, O my, how I toss and I turn,
I moan and I groan; I huff and I puff.
I take a deep breath and take a long sigh
Cause I am not with it today.

But then I grab my glasses and jump on up.
I make the bed, start the laundry,
fix the kids' breakfast, and clean the house
Cause I refuse to lay in bed all day, at least
Not today

I Can Only Think Of You

Sitting alone in my room
Thinking, not knowing what to do
Wondering who can I call on
'Cause I'm feeling down and blue.

> There's just nobody I can talk to
> All my family and friends don't have a
> clue
> Everyone seems to have other things to
> do
> Nobody knows what I'm going through.

I search to find someone to turn to
Falling down on my knees, I can only think of
you
Not knowing what to pray for
I begin to cry out, God, for help from You.

Shoo Fly!

You're the fly buzzing in my ear.
When I get you, you'll be dead.
No matter where I go, you're always there.

Every time I swing at you, I seem to miss.
Don't get me wrong, when I get my fly swatter
I'm sure it would love to give you a kiss.

So, you think you can just disappear.
I'll just wait a little while,
Then I will show you who lives here.

Looking out, you see none.
Wanting you, here I come.
With just one hit, it's all done.

Wait a minute, I know that's not another one...

Past-Present-Future

Show me what's worse.
Feeling like you know too much
Or looking like a total klutz.
Stepping back to give you room.
Taking advantage of what they know you do.
Looking back, you step in a trap.
Which causes you to become aware
Of the things that were always there.
Living life like there is no tomorrow.
Being careful not to borrow from the past
But to rely on the present to fuel the future...
Giving yourself a chance to breathe.
Realizing you are free to dream.
Understanding that it takes a little more effort to achieve
The things that seem so unreal to receive.
Giving yourself time to prove to yourself
That you can be who you want,
Go where you can
And do what you need.

Seconds

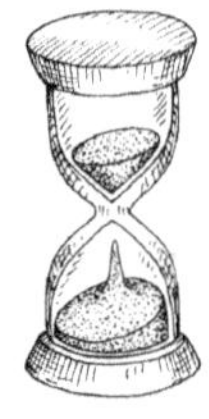

Don't blink, I promise you'll miss it.
Cause the way that time flies,
Every year that goes by feels like second
And in my mind, I'm trying to find the why.
Like, why is time going by so fast?
Why is my baby already nine, hitting ten.
It was just yesterday when I held him in my
arms.
In my mind, I'm wanting more time,
But hey, time waits for no one, right.

So don't blink, cause I promise you'll miss it.
As the years turn into months and the months
into weeks
And the weeks into days and the days into hours
It just makes it all seem like seconds.
So enjoy life and live in the moment.
Cause you don't want to miss it.
Keep a close eye on time so that you don't waste
It,
Because it all goes by in a matter of seconds.

Free My Mind

Can I tell you what's on my mind?
Can I trust you not to make me bawl?
Needing to desperately free my thoughts.
Needing, wanting to clear it all.
I'm holding it deep, deep within.
Holding back yesterday's fear and rejections.
It's way too heavy to keep inside.
It's now that I need your directions.
Accustomed to keeping it bottled away.
Accustomed to reminiscing on the past.
Please clear it all away.
Please clear me from thoughts fast.
Thoughts of what could have been.
Thoughts of what should have been.
Thoughts of what would have been.
Thoughts of what I feel inside,
Thoughts of what I don't understand.
Thoughts of what I need to say.
Thoughts of what I should do.
Thoughts of me and you.
Thoughts of where I should go.
Thoughts of right and wrong.
Thoughts of the unknown.
Consumed by thoughts running through my
head.

Holding in deep what needs to be said.

Side Effects

No more chocolate or caramel candy
    Just ginger chews for me
Cause every time I try to eat,
    It's nausea and an upset tummy.

Ginger ale and saltine crackers
    To settle the burning belly
Oh, how I long for the day to
    Just enjoy a peanut butter and jelly.

I dare not forget to mention,
    The side effect "cold dysesthesia."
So, nothing cold to drink or eat for me,
    Not even cookie dough ice cream.

Oh, I miss the days of pain-free eating.
    Just eat, drink, and chill.
But cancer and chemo have changed that,
    And all I feel is sick and ill.

But one day I will feel better,
    And be free from this pain.
To eat, laugh, and live.
    The jubilation I'd have gained.

A Dog Named Champ

A dog named Champ,
He was the best.
A golden retriever, boy was he ever amp.
Rolling round the hood, like he owned the
streets.
Scared a cat's bones right out of the meat.

Don't forget about the kids, man, you know what
I'm saying.
Champ sitting on the porch 'til about a quarter to
three.
Till the bus came a rolling and the kids came a
playing.

A very friendly dog.
Just liking the attention.
He had a very shiny coat.
No need to mention.

But it all came to an end
When they said he had to go.
That was a sad day,
The tears just wouldn't flow.

Now I'm missing my dog

Even though it's been a year.
No K-9 could ever replace him.
Man, I wish he was here.

Reach High My Boys

Reach for the stars, my boys.
It's yours for the taking.
Whatever you dream
I'm here to tell you,
that you can achieve.

Don't worry about the doubters.
They can't stop you.
The haters are there
to turn you but
They can't block you!

Your mama has your back.
I'll help you stay on track.
Your daddy will always be near.
So, don't you get caught up in fear.

Stand tall, my boys.
Keep your head held high.
With God by your side.
You can reach for the sky.

It's Hot

Gawd dang it's hot
So why am I sitting at this park?
The sweat beads formed on my low-shaved
head.
Water dipping down the side of my forehead.

Gawd dang it's hot.
Yet I'm sitting at this park.
Cause I got two kids, Yeah
two very active boys, to be exact,
and I'll do anything to keep them off my back.

Gawd dang it's hot
At this dang park.
My mouth is parched,
But the kids are having fun.

Gawd dang it's hot
Y'all know I'm at this park
Watching my boys play with
Their younger cousins.
These kids must not know it's hot.

Gawd dang it's hot.
So, why am I sitting at this park?
Cause my sister invited me and the boys
To enjoy some pizza and play.
On this last Friday of summer break.
And we had a good time at the park.

Always and Forever

I will love you always and forever
Even through the stormy weather
Whatever the consequence may be
Forever you will be with me
Through sunshine and rain
Heartache and pain
Always and forever we shall remain

You Can't Stay

You came to me o how did you find me?
You want to take over my body,
But I can't let you stay.

I pray and pray, for strength I pray,
To make it through day by day.
I will not let fear consume me.
I will not let cancer take me.

O the anxiety that comes
From so many doctor appointments.
The bloodwork and scans,
The poison they pump into my veins.

Let The Kids Be Kids

Let the kids be kids.
Let them run and play.
Let them make mistakes.
Let them learn along the way.

Let the kids be kids.
Let them sing and dance.
Let them yell and shout.
Let them take their stance.

Let the kids be Kids.
Let them be free.
Let them laugh and giggle.
Let their faces light up with glee.

Let the kids be kids.
Let them enjoy every moment.
Let them be happy and full of life.
Let their hearts be merry and content.

Faith

The substance of things hoped for
The evidence of things not seen
I don't think twice about breathing
The air that I feel is there but haven't seen it
I know that it's no goodness of mine that I'm
still here
I've been through plenty of things that could
have taken me out
Out naturally, out spiritually, or just out mentally
But my faith in God has delivered me

I'm here to please God but it's hard to do
Or so it seems, though His word says it's
impossible to do without faith
So, every day I put it to the test, yes, I've
Grown that mustard seed faith into something
great
Moving mountains that are meant to hold me
back
Blocking my path, trying to take me off track
But I know without a doubt that nothing is
impossible with God

Good Night

On the night of the busiest day,
When you go to lay your head, I pray
That you find the most peaceful sleep,
And your dreams are pure and sweet.

May sleep come to you swiftly this night.
May your eyes be heavy and breath be light.
May your mind be clear.
So that you sleep soundly, my dears.

With your body relaxed, with your mind clear.
The soft hum of the fan is all you hear.
With your angels keeping watch over you.
Have a good night, and remember, I love you!

Don't Let It Drop

The ball is dropping
And I have a choice
To either catch it or
Let it drop to the floor.

Now should I let it fall
There is no going back
Because once the ball drops
It will shatter once it cracks.

This ball of love,
That is what I'm rambling about.
It's complicated, to say the least.
But it can be very beautiful, no doubt.

This choice is not mine
Or then maybe it is
Do I catch it, wait for you to catch it,
Or shall I pack up and leave.

Do I want to be right
Or do I want to be married?
Do I catch the ball
Or do I give up on it all.

The Truth Before the Lie

If they say the truth hurts
Then they've never heard a lie
Cause I declare when it comes to a lie
The truth is always better.

They once tried to spare my feelings.
And decided to tell a lie.
But when I found out the truth, I was hurt.
Not because of what they lied about
But hurt because they felt they had to lie.

So, it has occurred to me.
It is better not to spare my feelings
But to always tell the truth
Because I can take the truth
But it must come before the lie.

Would you know?

What if I never touched you the way that made
you feel good?

If I didn't stare into your brown eyes.
Would you still think it was all good,
That I was feeling you just as much?

If I walked around and didn't stop to savor your
aroma.

If my body was never close to yours.
Wouldn't you wonder if I thought I was yours?

If I didn't talk to you with softness and calamity.
If I yelled all the time and didn't care how you
felt.
Would you still think I loved you with all my
heart?

What if I loved you as much as I do now
But never showed you or made you feel it.
If I never said it… Would you still know it?

Invisible

See me, hear me; I am not there.
I stand in the midst of a crowded room.
I watch, I listen, I do not move
They see me not because they don't care
My voice is loud or so I thought
But answer me, they did not.
I waved my hands in sight of their eyes.
I clapped, I stomped, though invisible am I.

Don't Let Him In

Don't open the door
Don't let Him in
He will steal your smile
And leave you with a frown
He will disrupt your peace
That you worked so hard to reach
He will destroy the order that you have placed.
He came to kill you; that is his fill,
And he will, if you open the door and let him in.

We Are Pets

What if we are just someone's pet
In this large cage called Earth.
Adults work until they sweat
Children run and play all day.

What if we are just someone's pet
But who then is our owner?
For which we provide
Companionship and pleasure.

What if we are just someone's pet
Submitting to our keeper
Giving it our best shot
To surrender ourselves to them.

Anger

The muscles in my body tighten like lug nuts on
an overly secured tire.
My breath is shortening with every puff of air I
try to inhale.
My chest is tight as I fight to keep it in, but the
anger I feel is starting to
boil over like a pot of hot grits.
The temperature change is like a house on fire
ignited by the disdain
treatment constantly bestowed upon me.
Though I can't blow, not today.
So, I breathe long and deep.
I calm myself before it escalates.
So, for now, the heat is turned down,
But I know the pressure is steadily building.
I know I need to find a permanent release.